39 POEMS

39 POEMS

John Ciardi

RUTGERS UNIVERSITY PRESS
New Brunswick, New Jersey, 1959

Library of Congress Catalogue Number: 59–15628

Acknowledgment is due the following magazines in which some of these poems first appeared: American Scholar, The Atlantic, Grecourt Review, The Literary Review, The Nation, Patterns, Poetry, A Magazine of Verse, Prairie Schooner, Quarterly Review of Literature, Saturday Review, Think, Venture

Manufactured in the United States of America by
H. Wolff, New York

Second Printing

For Charles E. Feinberg,
to name a man

Contents

I IN EGO WITH US ALL

II IN THE YEAR OF THE LONGEST CADILLAC

III CERTAINTIES

Part I

IN EGO WITH US ALL

i

Once I had 1000 roses.
Literally 1000 roses.
I was working for a florist
back in the shambling 'Thirties
when iced skids of 250 roses
sold for $2 at Faneuil Hall.
So for $8 I bought
1000 roses, 500
white and 500 red,
for Connie's wedding to steadiness.

I strewed the church aisle whole
and the bride came walking
on roses, roses all the way.
The white roses and the red roses.
White for the bed we had shared.
Red for the bed she went to
from the abundance in her
to the fear in what she wanted.
The gift was not in the roses
but in the abundance of the roses.

                                         To her
whose abundance had never wholly
been mine, and could never be his.
He had no gift of abundance in him
but only the penuries of sobriety.
A good steady clerk, most mortgageable,
returning in creaking shoes over

the white and the red roses. Returning
over the most flowering he would ever
touch, with the most flowering I
had ever touched. A feast of endings.

ii
This morning I passed a pushcart
heaped with white carnations
as high as if there had fallen all night
one of those thick-flaked, slow, windless,
wondering snows that leave
shakos on fence posts, polar bears
in the hedges, caves in the light,
and a childhood on every sill.
Once, twice a year, partially,
and once, twice a lifetime, perfectly,

that snow falls. In which I ran
like a young wolf in its blood
leaping to snap the flower-flakes
clean from the air; their instant on the tongue
flat and almost dusty and not enough
to be cold. But as I ran, face-up,
mouth open, my cheeks burned
with tears and flower-melt,
and my lashes were fringed with gauze,
and my ears wore white piping.

There is no feast but energy. All men
know—have known and will remember

again and again—what food that is
for the running young wolf of the rare days
when shapes fall from the air
and may be had for the leaping.
Clean in the mouth of joy. Flat and dusty.
And how they are instantly nothing—
a commotion in the air and in the blood.
—And how they are endlessly all.

iii

My father's grave, the deepest cave I know,
was banked with snow and lilies.
We stuck the dead flowers
into the snow banks dirty with sand
and trampled by digger's boots.
The flowers, stiff and unbeckoning,
ripped from their wires in the wind
and blew their seasons out as snow.
Purer than the snow itself. A last
abundance correcting our poverties.

I remember the feasts of my life,
their every flowing. I remember
the wolf all men remember in his blood.
I remember the air become
a feast of flowers. And remember
his last flowers whitening winter
in an imitation of possibility,
while we hunched black

5

in the dirtied place inside possibility
where the prayers soiled him.

If ever there was a man of abundances
he lies there flowerless
at that dirty center
whose wired flowers try and try
to make the winter clean again in air.
And fail. And leave me raging
as the young wolf grown
from his day's play in abundance
to the ravening of recollection.
Creaking to penury over the flower-strew.

iv

This morning I passed a pushcart
heaped beyond possibility,
as when the sun begins again
after that long snow and the earth
is moonscaped and wonderlanded
and humped and haloed in the
light it makes: an angel
on every garbage can, a god
in every tree, that childhood
on every sill.—At a corner of the ordinary.

Where is she now? Instantly nothing.
A penury after flower-strew. Nothing.
A feast of glimpses. Not fact itself,

but an idea of the possible in the fact.
—And so the rare day comes: I was again
the young wolf trembling in his blood
at the profusions heaped and haloed
in their instant next to the ordinary.
And did not know myself what feast I kept
—till I said your name. At once all plenty was.

It is the words starve us, the act that feeds.
The air trembling with the white wicks
of its falling encloses us. To be
perfect, I suppose, we must be brief.
The long thing is to remember
imperfectly, dirtying with gratitude
the grave of abundance. O flower-banked,
air-dazzling, and abundant woman,
though the young wolf is dead, all men
know—have known and must remember—
                    You.

A Dream

I had a dream once of dancing with a tiger. As it took
    my arm off, I heard a dancing-master
who came by on a bus with his dancing class on an outing
    say to the class:
"Note and avoid this dancer's waste of motion—more
    violence than observance."
And as I died and woke, I heard him add: "Dancing, my dears,
    is a selection of measures."

Once at St. Joseph's, asked by Father Ryan something I have
    forgotten, I answered, burning,
something I meant for love. He grabbed my hair and hauled
    me to the Virgin.
"Pray for your soul!" But I stomped my heel on his instep
    and ran damned
my first long race from God, to hide by the river till
    I dared go home and be strapped.

I was what had been done to me. There in the grass
    I lay outside my action.
Whose was the act? Whose will, not mine, was in it?
    How was it chosen
that the thing done had been given me to do? I envied the birds
    the eyes they could eat from my head
for a little waiting. I lay already dead in God's eye
    upon me.

You think perhaps it's a child's tale, that nose of
    Pinocchio's?

All boys are born of the guilt that sprouts from them
    in a wrong world
whose Virgins and Good Fairies accept prayers, tears,
    and apologies
from the block-head who becomes a man at last by the act
    of cutting his nose off.

There in the river reeds, outside of God and the happening
    act, I learned
my tiger to dream to. When I laid my face in the river
    to cool my tears
a rat swam under my eyes, no further away than this paper.
    And came swimming
into a thousand dreams I screamed from. Rat? Tiger? I
    forget now which was which.

But that dancing-master—why had my face been put
    between his wig and ruffles?
Which of my acts was done to me so in secret that I
    wake here
at forty in a white shirt and a striped coat of manners,
    and bow and bow,
teaching the children songs and kisses and curtsies,
    to one side of all tigers in my arms?

In Ego with Us All

In ego with us all, behind the world and Mother,
in the woods behind the house, where the old well is
for everyone to remember, I remember
the stone-green water's far-down breathing over
the lead-gold-emerald frog that shines there
when the light goes high enough to find him.

It was the Secret Place. Jesse James came there,
Babe Ruth, Charlie Chaplin, Captain Nemo.
And when the light fell deepest, Pa came smiling:
"See, I'm not dead: show me what's in the well."
Then how the frog sang up from the stones and water,
sweet as canaries, and golden in our look!

Till a bell clanged it to lead. "All right, I'm coming!"
It was The Lonely Place, bell-emptied in a wink,
even the Frog gone, which was again only
the round stone I had dropped, both arms extended
over the center to aim it true and forever.
And counted all my nights to the sound of the splash.

And never heard it. In ego with us all
I think there is no hearing it. It is dropped,
it lies there, it changes when the light lets it.
But no one hears it hit. Is it forever
the bell clangs just at that instant?
Are the clang and the splash one sound neither

Father nor Mother, but both? I do not know
what there is of us in that well that dreamed me

through light and dark. The thought is years from the thought,
and our lives are not a thing chosen but a thing
that happens to us. Out of that well, perhaps.
Out of it or another impossibility, certainly.

I have let go my tears for less than this.
Even at movies, damning myself for a fool,
I have leaked sentiment for dead dolls.
Who are you? Have you a drier eye?—
In ego with us all, I confess all:
there is no world but what falls in that well,

sings out when the light goes high enough, sinks off
to slime and stone between. And the thought
lies years from the thought. The Lonely Place
is the ruins of The Secret Place. The True is quiet:
leaves nudge it, grasshoppers fizz in it, water laps it,
the singing comes up from the well—the voice of Quiet.

And years from all, in ego with us all, as I have shed
with all of us, damning for all of us, the wrong
tears for not-enough reason, I will sit tending
the silence coldly told of what tears are true
in ego with us all, in the secret place
a noise can shatter, and a life not mend.

Palaver's No Prayer

PALAVER'S no prayer.
There's a nice-ninny priest
at tea in everyone,
all cosy and chatty as auntie,
but a saint comes
and throws rocks through the window.

In Place of a Curse

At the next vacancy for God, if I am elected,
I shall forgive last the delicately wounded
who, having been slugged no harder than anyone else,
never got up again, neither to fight back,
nor to finger their jaws in painful admiration.

They who are wholly broken, and they in whom
mercy is understanding, I shall embrace at once
and lead to pillows in heaven. But they who are
the meek by trade, baiting the best of their betters
with the extortions of a mock-helplessness

I shall take last to love, and never wholly.
Let them all into Heaven—I abolish Hell—
but let it be read over them as they enter:
"Beware the calculations of the meek, who gambled nothing,
gave nothing, and could never receive enough."

A Look of Understanding

He turned to face me, barely nodding, wryly,
and suddenly his eyes were more than his.
Or maybe less than his. But no longer one man's eyes,
no longer in a face even. Or, rather, his face—
the particularity of his slightly tired,
mildly bumped and hollowed, one, human face—
faded, and something like a generalized face
that could do for anyman's and was everyman's
contained those eyes, and the eyes took possession
of that face, dimming it to a suggestion,
to a half-sketched allusion through which
the presence of his eyes declared itself.

At a showing of famous jewels once
I saw stones from fabulous strikes
and others with no known beginning,
blazing and changeless from a thousand hands,
and the throats of powerful women dead, and the crowns
and string-works of Empires with no name.
There sat the stones, evident and unlosable,
their thousand possessors faded from them.
A memory like the shadow round a shining.

His eyes were like those stones
from which generations can only fade,
changing nothing from the evident and unlosable
first blazing within them
to the last flesh from which they would sink
into the earth again, to be found or not.

Shark Hunter

By flashlight under the covers
in the hobgoblin nights
of my bloody first hunger
for everything—there,
in the cave safe from Mother,
I read my eyes out of my head
in my own light to a light beyond,
in which, blood-pistons pounding,
I loved—oh, more than God—
      Shark Hunter.

Ah, not even the natives eyed him
as I did inside myself.
Kuamoto sent him his own daughter
to lie with. And when the traders
stole the jeweled eye and fled, who
dove from Luago's edge,
outswam their sails, and hauled them—
captain and crew—to thrash
paid-for in the snakepit? Who but
      Shark Hunter?

See him there, great-thewed tumbler
through red bubbles under the shark's belly,
his knife at a slit in Genesis, his blood
outpounding the giant squid's pulse
on dark bottoms, his hail
rising from surf in the first dusk
home from the beaten sea.
Then how the maidens lei'd him!

bringing their flowers like torches to
    Shark Hunter!

That was a born imagination
those nights in my flowerless first cave
beyond Mother. Whoever it was
lived days to mind her, I
rolled in red foam and gambled
my life in lusts, killing, because I dared,
the torrential shark, and rising
as He rose from shore-seethe
to tower in garlands for me, my
    Shark Hunter!

After Sunday Dinner
We Uncles Snooze

Banana-stuffed, the ape behind the brain
scratches his crotch in nature and lies back,
one arm across his eyes, one on his belly.
Thanksgiving afternoon in Africa,
the jungle couches heaped with hairy uncles
between a belch and a snore. All's well that yawns.

Seas in the belly lap a high tide home.
A kind of breathing flip-flop, all arrival,
souses the world full in the sog of time,
lifting slopped apes and uncles from their couches
for the long drift of self to self. Goodbye:
I'm off to idiot heaven in a drowse.

This is a man. This blubbermouth at air
sucking its flaps of breath, grimacing, blowing,
rasping, whistling. Walked through by a zoo
of his own reveries, he changes to it.
His palm's huge dabble over his broken face
rubs out the carnivores. His pixie pout

diddles a butterfly across his lip.
His yeasty smile drools Edens at a spring
where girls from Bali, kneeling to their bath,
cup palms of golden water to their breasts.
His lower lip thrusts back the angry chiefs:
he snarls and clicks his teeth: "Stand back, by God!"

And so, by God, they do, while he descends
to rape those knobs of glory with a sigh,   17

then clouds, surceased, and drifts away or melts
into another weather of himself
where only a drowned mumble far away
sounds in his throat the frog-pond under time.

O apes and hairy uncles of us all,
I hear the gibberish of a mother tongue
inside this throat. (A prattle from the sea.
A hum in the locked egg. A blather of bloods.)
O angels and attendants past the world,
what shall the sleeps of heaven dream but time?

For Bernard DeVoto

A thumb and a forefinger on the eyes
draw down the light: the fact that teaches all
shuts at the lid. That last hand still in air,
not yet, nor ever, wholly returned from its gesture,
changes to a dead weight across the heart.
Goodbye to seeing and goodbye from sight.

This was a man. This lump in the numb blank
of bedsheets, hours, losses. Like a tide
his warmth sinks from the mud-edge of his blood.
His interrupted face above that tide
turns to a blue-veined marble one firm hour,
then shudders liquid to the end of time.

Wolves, eagles, fishes, angels—when they dared—
have died into that sea. Leviathans and cells
have burst from their stiff last across that mud.
So must a man be what the sea takes back.
But here, and for the man-hour of a thought,
it is an admiration stuns the sea.

What shall the sea in all its driven pumps
cast up from its pearl chambers in the sun
more than the man it takes? More than the run
of the infinite small waters of his brain
away from their stilled systems in the gulf?
To name a man is to give birth to nature.

Sea that drains all dregs, drains this. Goodbye.
This was a man, and I will swear his name

whole as I may from my own name and losses.
I knew no fault in him I could not love.
I find no death in us but justifies.
One deep is all, and its one shore—a man.

It Is the Same Place
Always Once Again

The most truth of what is most usual
can be spoken backwards only and only after
some part of all is finished. Zinnias,
in their commonplace rank blazes bordering
a day, are a color of something/nothing,
glad and ordinary to the eye that accepts thanks.
. . . But that you will never again be the hand that plants,
nor the step between them on the walk—*that*
is the one measure of the going of all color.

The hedge grows wild or is trimmed by another.
Come twilight and star-twitch, the young lions prowl again
up the same walk to the same step, and there,
like a moonrise in the doorway, a girl
who could almost be you, waits, glowing and sudden.
They do not know what they will have to remember—
not she in her power, nor they in their dance around it—
and therefore they believe only
the extraordinary of themselves, and cannot hear

when they stroll melded in poolside shadows
how I whisper of you behind them,
wishing them the great tremor and tenderness
of your body again as they at last must find it
if ever they may learn to endure in themselves
their returning and returning past the same hedge
in its other hands, the border of zinnias
doused in darkness, the door of their night kiss turning,
from which they turn once, and never again.

The One Dull Thing You Did
Was to Die, Fletcher

for Fletcher Pratt

To you, Fletcher, from my dark house asleep
in the sound of its lives breathing, at three
of a tired morning, and, as it happens,
in Rome—which could be Oslo or Shanghai
to any sense of mine: a place like any,
a distance equally anywhere from you
engraved in your dull death—and a damn poor likeness. . . .

I read a fool's book late, then puttered
along a marble hall a block long nowhere
at a hundred-thousand lire a month, and poured
my last shot of real Armagnac.
                         And now,
here I stand, a sheep-face in the mirror,
the drink raised in this crazy Italian dim
of every bulb too small for what it does
and everyone saving a lira the wrong way.

Here I stand in this light that sticks to shadow
without half changing it, and there you are
as long as rent, and time wherever *it* is
in a lira's worth of something saved from dying.
God, what a silly way to keep a budget!
Well, here goes: from your budget's end and mine,
the last of what there is—to you, Fletcher,
maudlin, but in the best that money can buy.

To Dudley Fitts

(Some mortal lines while lying in bed
with a jangling sacro-iliac)

Patience, Dudley, we are two dried paltries.
Two sticks of season bloating at the bark.
Think what it is to think and still to be
at the stick-end of economy in the same wood
where once there were not thighs enough to squander!
But smile, old hobbled horse, days are worth something:
that smile at least, a head cocked to old jazz.

Or should we go down solemn and unbudged,
toga'd in our own fat like statuary?
as heavy set as those last senators
who sat in their stone places to the end
as if at Law, while through the balanced arches
the redbeards lurched to topple-in the day?
It *is* an Empire we outsit at last.

Or should we rail back moon-mad, damning all?
—I lie in bed, the ape-tail at my spine's end
jangling a buzzer of pain at my least stir:
part of a bedpan reading Robert Browning.
Bah! I wish I had the Henry Miller
I smuggled in from Paris but lent and lost.
It takes a madman to see all the moon.

But patience, patience. I smile at the madman's children
caroming in and out; bless his bright wife,
her flower trays of surprises and hot broth;
pat her behind, a melon from the moon;

lie naked to be washed, feeling her hands
soft as a birth's first night-knock at the womb.
—I drift toward my own embryo in sleep.

If death has such small hands, why, let it in:
some idiot snuggle at the pit of day
wriggles from self into the opium rot
that clings to all wet rooting where the dead
let out their gas of life to be first food.
Idiot sweet, I drowse there till the buzzer
grates once more at the ape-end of the spine.

Jangled awake and bursting at the bladder,
I reach for the goose-neck: gone to tidiness.
Damned if I'll yell for help: twinge and be damned.
But minutes later my wife comes sweetly clucking
to find me stiff and sweating on all fours,
stranded in my own hall like some obese
and stinking hound at its arthritic end.

Thank you. Thank you. Thank you. Thank you. Sorry.
I knew I shouldn't have, but I had to try.
Thank you, darling. Easy. All right. Now.
She gets me turned about and inch by inch
eases me back into a hotpad's rat's-nest,
a scolding mercy gentling me to bed.
It is the same bed in the same day's glare.

It is the same smile softening at the end:
patience in love, a coddle for a fool.

So am I changed to drizzle in the same field
where once I was all thunder. *Mop me, love.*
But if you dare forget the nights this bed
bucked in the moon . . . but if you dare forget. . . .
Ah, Senator, senators remember Rome!

. . . Paltries, Dudley, we are two shrunk paltries.
But bless us both, and for a sort of blessing
I trace this invalid drifting of the light.
That dead dog in the hallway sniffs through time
to its rooty end in the stiff sweat of damn.
Easy does it. Take this prattle for praise,
Old Paltry Bones, these two sticks clacked together.

Bridal Photo, 1906

A ceremonial rose in the lapel
a horseshoe wreath of pearls in the tie-knot,
a stone-starched collar bolted at the throat,
a tooth on a gold chain across the vest—
this is the man, costumed for solemn taking.

Pompadoured and laced and veiled for giving,
the woman sits her flower-time at his side
badged with his gifts—gold watch on a fleur-de-lis
pin at the heart, gold locket at the throat—
her hand at total rest under his hand.

What moment is this frozen from their lives
as if a movie stuck in its lit tracks?

Between the priest's gilt cave and their new bed,
ducking and giggling through the rowdy friends
who scattered rice and waited to get drunk,

they ran out of their day to the rigged cave
of the unknown hooded man who took their look
and made it into paper. Here they are:
stopped with all eyes upon them in his eye,
so solemn and so starched, they must have laughed

a thousand times, when they could laugh again,
to see themselves carved from themselves like stone.
And yet what moment is this of their lives
who hold their lives so open to all looking?
Was this the bridal and all else the dance?

Half-man, half-woman, not yet one another,
but in a first time and a last between
that separate morning and all joined good nights,
they stood to think their lives into one look
and hold the unfinished bridal to its hour.

Oh man and woman tranced in your new flowers,
your eyes are deep as churches, but as far
as you look out unseeing, the years look in!
Sweet strangers, I am left across your lives
to see the flower day taken from its flowers.

I follow this long look into its dark
where, leathered as an Indian chief, the woman
sags through this lace to keen for the bashed corpse
that drops from the man's steadiness in his hour.
I hold this study by the hooded man

and pray to that held hour from its last love:
    Bless the unfinished bridal to its bed.
    This day becomes this day. What others follow
    have touched their flower. By all flowers and all fall
    I am the son of this man and this woman.

Part II

IN THE YEAR OF THE
LONGEST CADILLAC

Washington, D.C.

In the year of the longest Cadillac,
from picture windows in the heart,
to the rosebud and cherry-tree

rim of the stone-and-iron Wheel of Embassies
there by the Potomac, and in God's name, came
The Regency of Evasion.

Kings of Texas and of Detroit
convoyed the Bald Head smiling on its pillow.
Jet trails spumed and spelled

His name to heaven in the upper airs
that howled and twisted it. The writing
squatted and stretched blue.

So the unlettering wind flapped all the rim,
but the Head rode prompted and propped
to the stone-domed Hub

where Reporters waited, and the Cameras
had stared through their stanchions for days,
their pictures already inside them.

Oh marvelous how he resembled
the picture the cameras brought up like a cud
from their stored contentment!

Marvelous how the voice taped into the pillow
spoke in time to the motion of the lips
with scarcely a twitch visible!

And if any man swear me to politics
for what I say here, accusing me
of a vote that sneers,

I say to that man: graves and breadbaskets
open and close as those lips open and close;
that Wheel of Embassies

began and ends again in Adam's wages
and Eve's tongue knotted in her mouth to stammer
her language of tears;

but these are tongueless men at the center,
and of their damnations that avoid the name
the fruit slurs rotten out of every tree.

Inscriptions for a Soldier's Marker ✓

i

Reasoning as my people reasoned, I stared
with God from a gunsight, praising Him whole
for the man I killed. His blood is not restored

except by blood. I learned in the grapnel fields
that the best of us is danger. Praise Him
who holds the dead boy and enfolds

the leg blown from its body. When I fell,
deeper than grass His name dunned all the ground.
For as much as I understood, I paid in full.

ii

Behaviour and Sin were my father and mother.
   I was born to the Civil War of Gland and Guilt,
   fought on both sides, was killed impartially.

Was there another way past birth? I lost it.
   War made me and outlived me. The bone skills
   of a conscript generation shaped me from blood.

I watched mud-bearded boys go goddamning
   into the crossfire over the heaving ridge,
   or throw themselves like bone dice on the gun-nest,

or hold the split plane to its course wisecracking
   tits and twats. I understood a kind
   of purification unspeakable to all

but the sure dead. I learned by easy bones
to commit my refusal. Consenting and immortal,
the living perjured their own way to Hell.

Letter from Paris

In Paris they remember Paris was there before Christ.
This is not an important memory in Rome. It *is*
a memory, to be sure, but among other business.

In Paris talk comes slower and with longer pauses.
On parade days there is much wiping of eyes
as the flag passes. The young are mad for *le jazz hot*.

There is something and nothing inside seventy million
French memories, moods, and pre-occupations
that stands forever at windows into a twilight.

"*Nous sommes foutus!*" cries the *café* philosopher
after two hours of nursing a *demi-bière*.
"*Nous sommes français!*" jerks the barmaid, but it hangs
there—

a clumsy reflex. A self-evident unanswerable
self-evidently unanswered, even by the last *élève*
and the last before it and the last before it stumbling

blood-stubbled in the sunburst dunes to no end,
and the bottom scraped. "Morocco? That *is* France!"
And the Deputies cheer. But the *café* falls silent

except for the billiard balls clicked by two Norwegians,
and an hour's comma later in the same conversation
the philosopher answers her: "*Et puis foutus!*"   35

It is very much to remember everything that must be
remembered today in Paris. The best of men
suddenly, between *demi* and *demi*, is caught in a fog-filled

speculation most like a dawn-mist in the Colosseum.
Something in Paris is changing memories faster
than all the stones can hold. Or the stones are breathing.

The mist walks up one alley and another.
At the *Vieux Colombier* across the mist
les amateurs dig-dig le Muskrat Ramble.

Of History, Fiction, Language

Just as no one works for a living in Oscar Wilde,
and practically no one does in Henry James,
so there are histories that eat no bread, or not enough;

and others that are bread alone, or armies alone,
or mistresses alone, or diplomats alone and none that, suffi-
    ciently,
eat, fight, bounce baby, and talk six dialects at once.

My daughter, at one, discovered that the negative of O.K.
is No-K, and Victoria (somewhat older, but only that)
discovered and said: "We (meaning 'my Us-ness') are not
    amused,"

which, coming from an Us-ness was automatically an Of
    Course,
but added what to the resources of the language? Whereas
my daughter is tongue enough for all futures. And she is mine,

recorded in this history and no other. A scoop.
A people with enough daughters in their memory
will not vote wrong. May she correct Election. I

swear here by Persian Peloponnesian and Punic that no
bugle ever in time called to its commonplace troopings
any but private fathers of the Extraordinary,

lovers of ineluctable Herselfs, and unique sons of Places, who,
ranked in the lie-agreed-upon, one hour on stage
did nothing much, and all their lives in the wings

put meanings to the tongues that utter kings.   37

After the Street Fighting

For the First Anniversary of the
Hungarian Revolution of October 1956.

i

After the street fighting their tanks pull back for the night
And the women come turning the dead over, hunched and
   swaying,
black as buffalo in a dried river bed
swinging from sniff to sniff at the last mud
and waiting in the only place they know.

Then one by one they stiffen human; their faces
lean sidewise and down with the eyes sagged over
and the mouths ripped. The bread falls from their hands,
always the same. They kneel
by the mud of the corpse as if by living water.

You do nothing. You have earned your separation.
The women kneel and pot the mud of the dead
in their arms and bear its black blooming.
You wait for your own woman, her slow surprise
like the broken bread in her hand, wormy and edible.

You do nothing. Your jaws eat. It is already
tomorrow in her eyes. It is yourself
turned over by the women with the bread
stoned from their fists. You are dead and owe no one
this last look for the night at your own corpse.

Either you do not care or what you care for
is already over. She would give herself in the rubble

you know, and later you will take her,
but now it is all a life
to touch her cheek once with your finger tips.

Your jaws eat for you. There is nothing to say.
One by one the women bear their corpses.
Either you do not care or what you care for
is already over. The silence tastes
of dust and plaster. And later you will take her.

ii

"My darling," you think, as if practicing to be human,
"Oh may your door be open from this death!"
But there is nothing to imagine. There is between you,
better than hope, the fact that your deaths have been paid for.
From the death that pays in advance there are no doors.

There is only the right to remain separate once more
from the flowers of the black women, to eat bread
with the jaws of the dead man, to touch—
as if it mattered—her cheek with your fingers,
to wait the easing in of night on the rubble.

You think: "I have never been purer than this.
Not in rose-childhood nor the lily sacraments,
nor taking the bread from my mouth for a cackling beggar,
nor high on the sweaty brawl of the walloped harvest,
nor in the first great moonlight of her bed."

iii

To be alive after you have been paid for
is someways a confusion. You know your death,
but habit strolls loose in another contract.
Glance away from the signature even an instant
and memory shuffles the papers as if for living.

Your mind waits among its deceptions that do not
deceive. You watch it play like children in themselves.
An indulgence that could even be joy removes you:
let the nerve stir its last: let it be wrong
lovingly a little. Either you do not care

or what you care for is already
over. You lie at your own feet,
your mouth a bomb of flies. You think: "Sometime
someone may use these deaths." But what does it matter?
Tomorrow must solve itself. To be alive
after you have been paid for is the confusion:

that last night in the rubble, as if for love.

For Giordano Bruno's Monument
in the Campo dei Fiori

Burned at the stake by the
Inquisition, February 17, 1600

A game of shanks those saints play, nibble tibia.
Pull the bloody rug out from under.
Then in prattfall shall the man become.

Mix me a dialect, Giordano Bruno,
for the Roman snap of flames in the manface,
the Florentine lisp of faggots, the holy vowel

of the pushed air through drafts in the manskin.
All tongues can damn: "Look at a Universe, will you?
We'll show you stars!" Spin me that treatise, Bruno,

of the firewalk into God a man is
for having thought to think. And how the game
is played to bone from bonfires in man's dark.

Leave me a tongue to speak to all gravespill
the name of a broiler that was once a man
by passion, mathematics, and philosophy

—and split to cracklings. That when next I stand
knee deep in the wire-stuck rose and the tribal ribbon
bedding a dead man to his time of oozes,

I may know better men have thudded wet
as a horsequarter to the den floor, or soiled
as a burnt roast to garbage, leaving

man's tongue confused to meat, and still—
bursting from carrion like a gull surprised—
the sprung word's wingspread taking all the air.

Ballad of the Icondic

It was the year the ICONDIC
  was sighted (hush, my pet,
for it has slewn the GAWNOSE WATT
  and it is slewing yet).

It was THEOLGARD shook its head.
  THENOOGARD likewise its.
And having knit a BITTAPPEASE
  they raveled it to snits.

"Now what shall save us?" ICONDIC
  cried out, as if in thought.
"O gird about your gat, set out
  and slew the GAWNOSE WATT!"

The GAWNOSE WATT it slew and slew.
  Was never seen such slewage.
And GAWNOSE WATT went up the spout.
  And GAWNOSE WATT went down the sewerage.

I only know the ICONDIC
  slewed on and still is slewing.
(Now sleep, and may you dream just what
  the GAWNOSE WATT was doing.)

A Dialogue in the Stoneworks

Said the Curator of Easy Dying
to the Auditor of Knuckle Bones,
"There's a move afoot, I'm thinking.
A man can feel it coming."

"Um," said the Auditor counting the Medes and Persians,
"Why not? With nothing to do and only
his jug for a premise, why shouldn't a sot
feel any damn thing he's a mind to?"

"Ah well," said the Curator,
"and if it's my personal bad flavor
at issue, why I may stink with the best,
but I feel a truth, and all will."

"Truth?" said the Auditor starting the middle Egyptians.
"Is it a dry truth or wet?
Can a sober man feel it, I say,
as well as a sot—who shall be nameless, I say?"

"Doubts," said the Curator of Easy Dying.
"Doubts and dirty implications.
Haven't I granted you all you could wish
concerning my character? I feel a thing beyond me."

"Ha," said the Auditor, "barely five measly million:
just as I always claimed." And began the Etruscans,
who were finished almost at once.
"Call that a breed now?" he said.

"It's nothing to do," said the Curator swigging deep
and wiping a sigh from his mouth wet,
"with what an add-man can count to.
We're coming to countless days, I tell you."

"So," said the Auditor clicking the Greco-Sicilians,
"technological unemployment! Some day when I've time
you must let me explore for myself
that jug of dream juice."

"Scoff," said the Curator of Easy Dying.
"There's big times coming.
I tell you these vaults won't hold it
once it gets started."

"And," said the Auditor, ticking Sardinia, "what if it *is*
true, and the knuckles spill over the lawn
and into the ditch? Swig on, you sot, and let it.
Whatever it is, I'll know it when I count it."

S.P.Q.R. A Letter from Rome

Sono Porci Questi Romani

i

It does for the time of man to walk here
by the spoken stones forgotten, a criss-crossed empire
sticking its stumps out of cypress. Not a name,
though stone-carved, but what a name
is plastered over it. Not a god in town
but watched his temple changed into a quarry.

And could smile: "Let them change Heaven and Earth
if they can: nothing changes the Romans.
Men as they were, beasts as they were, they are.
Their God across the Tiber has stone arms
stretched from his dome like crab's claws. Can claws hold
    them?
A thousand kings have held Rome; none, the Romans.

Who knows the goats better than the goatherd?
We piped their lambing from burnt rock
and made a people of them. Rank and graceless
they are a people yet. And ours. All arches
are one to them. Whatever name is on them,
they read their own. Exactly as we gave it."

—You hear that gods' pique everywhere. A jobless
immortality fallen to sneers and gossip.
They'll rob you blind, kick your shins bloody,
elbow you over the edge, then smile and say *"Scusi."*
History? Rome's no history, but a madhouse.
So, I suppose, the original of history.

It does for all of time to walk there
over the unchanged changes—like a guard mount,
the same before and after. What's there to change?
You go to the Vatican or the Pantheon
in the same mob.
                And keep your pockets buttoned:
leave one flap open—you'll learn history.

ii

On stone, her stoned knees throbbing like a pulse
in the concussion of holiness, Sister Pia,
vowed to meditation, unwashed, unflinching,
prayed in her stones that days and men be laundered.

"If I am worthy, teach me what I must suffer."
Ten years upon her knees in the odor of grace.
Spoon-fed a broth a day by those who cleaned her;
the prayer bubbling on through every spoonfull.

Ten years on her knees while the stone cell
became a Colosseum and the blood
steamed, hymned, to Heaven from the beasts'
muzzles and the glory was said and said.

"If I am worthy, bless them." And was tolled
by bells and the praying shadows of stone,
the Convent black with triumph. —While, at the gates,
a hundred thousand Fiats snarled and screeched.

iii

Till one claxon of all rang statues quick:
    Mussolini ha sempre ragione. And he came
    out of the stones like yesterday-made-easy.
    A new statue sprung from every footfall.

Empire! And the mob remembered! It rained stone chips
    in Rome all one generation as the masons swung
    again. A thousand, ten thousand, a million
    stone-thrust-chins for piazzas, dressers, export:

in the mud at Addis Ababa, an Arch of Triumph;
    in Libya, on the sand grill, a Colossus;
    across the Mare Nostrum in the moon,
    a bust of glory on the binnacle.

Till all hung upside-down on a northern wall,
    suffered as Sister Pia to its stones, and the mob
    sang: "*Fatto! Viva l'America!*" Turned, praying:
    "If I am worthy—Joe, a cigarette."

iv

It does for the time of all to walk here
    by the saved arches and the forgotten surrenders.
    An empire of ego figging its thumbs at heaven.
    A museum of famines lurking to snatch bread.
    A propriety of dressed scorns promenading.
    A cradle of prayer bubbling.

As time is. Half a nonsense. Like a guard mount:
the same stone godwatch before and after,
a grandiose serenity with its lips cracked,
smirking: "Let them change Heaven and Earth
if they can. Nothing changes a Roman."

And still a marble marriage pomps the light.

Massive Retaliation

Saipan 1944–1945.
Aerial Offensive Against Japan.

I gaped, admitted, at some of what we did
those days at skip-ocean, watching the shore towns blow
like spouts below us, staring into volcanoes
at the half-closed red eye under everything.

One moon-mist night six miles above Nagoya
we let our fish go, banked wide over mountains.
A searchlight from the world washed us in green,
lost us to black, returned, lost us again.

Those wars were all waiting. I waited, looking down
into the dark of one more thing set fire to.
Then we were over ocean and alive.
The blaze went out. We dove into the dawn.

It was as far from home as we could go.
I remember the teeth of the mountains of the moon
and the meteors falling in. By afternoon
it was official. Something had been done.

We acted boredom but lived better. Once,
above the sea, circling a rendezvous rock,
we filled the east and west with silver sharks
pinwheeling like a marriage race of gods.

It was a thousand of ourselves we saw.
A thousand theorems spiraled from the sun
to some proof statelier than the thing done.
A sky-wide silver coming of the Law.

Even toward murder such possibility
meets and becomes. Like empires on their shields
we circled over time, and the great wheel
blazed like a reason on the lighted sea.

I gaped for all good men at what we were,
dressed in such bridals, spilling from the sun,
stuffed with such thunderbolts, and come
so far from home, almost beyond return.

To Lucasta, About That War

A long winter from home the gulls blew
on their brinks, the tankers slid
over the hump where the wolf packs hid
like voodoo talking, the surf threw
bundles with eyes ashore. I did
what booze brought me, and it wasn't you.

I was mostly bored. I watched and told time
as enforced, a swag-man
under the clock. The bloat-bags ran
wet from nowhere, selling three-for-a-dime
and nobody buying. Armies can
type faster than men die, I'm

told, and can prove. Didn't I find
time there, and more, to count
all, triplicate, and still walk guard-mount
on the gull- and drum-wind
over the hump? I did, and won't
deny several (or more) pig-blind

alleys with doors, faces, dickers,
which during, the ships slid
over the hump where the packs hid.
And talking voodoo and snickers
over the edge of their welts, I did
what I could with (they called them) knickers;

and it was no goddamn good,
and not bad either. It

was war (they called it) and it lit
a sort of skyline somehow in the blood,
and I typed the dead out a bit
faster than they came, or anyone should,

and the gulls blew high on their brinks,
and the ships slid, and the surf threw,
and the Army initialed, and you
were variously, vicariously, and straight and with kinks,
raped, fondled, and apologized to—
which is called (as noted) war. And it stinks.

Ulysses

At the last mountain I stood to remember the sea
and it was not the sea of my remembering
but something from an augur's madness:
sheep guts, bird guts, ox guts, smoking
in a hot eye. Was this my life? Dull red,
dull green, blood black, the coils still writhing
the last of the living thing: a carnage
steaming into the smokes of a sick dawn.

I had planted the oar at the crossroads, there in the goat dust
where the oaf waited, chewing a stalk of garlic.
"Stranger," he said, "what have you on your shoulder?"
"A world," I said, and made a hole for it,
watched by the oaf and his goats. I gave him money
for the fattest goat and asked to be alone,
and he would not leave me. I gave him money again
for a peace-parting, and he would not go.
"Stranger," I said, "I have sailed to all lands,
killed in all lands, and come home poor. I think
blood buys nothing, and I think it buys
all that's bought. Leave me this goat and go."
Why should I want his blood on me? The goat
stared at me like an old man, and the oaf
sat chewing garlic. This much had been commanded.
Was the rest commanded, too? Was it my life
or the god's laughter foresaw me?

                                        I prayed in anger:
"O coupling gods, if from your lecheries
among the bloods of man, a prayer may move you

to spare one life, call off this last sad dog
you have set on me. Does Heaven need such meat?"
The heavens lurched on unheeding. The fool stayed:
would not be scared off, and would not be whipped off.
Then he raised his staff against me.

                                        Was it my life
or the gods' laughter answered? I hacked him sidearm
across the middle: almost a stunt for practice—
dead level, no body weight to it, all in the shoulder
and wrist, and not three feet to the whole swing.
But it halved him like a melon! A chop
the ships would have sung for a century!
. . . But there were no ships, and the oar was planted unknown
in a country of garlic and goat turds,
and what lay fallen was rags and bones.

                                  "Take him, then!" I cried.
"Who else could stomach such a dusty tripe?"
I made the pyre with the planted oar at its center,
and as it flamed, I raised the libation cup,
but mouthed the wine and spat it at the blaze.
The fire roared up like Etna. "At your pleasure!"
I shouted back, and threw the dead clown in,
first one piece, then the other. The horns of the flame
raped him whole and blew for more. The goats
stood watching, huddled like old crazy men
in a chorus round the fire, and one by one
I slit their throats and threw them to their master.
I say those goats were mad: they waited there

as if the fire were Medusa: the blood of the dead
ran down the legs of the living and they did not move,
not even to turn their heads. And in the center
the flame went blood-mad in a shaft to Heaven.

It was dark when I turned away. I lost my road
and slept the night in a grove. When I awoke
I found a shrine to Apollo, a marble peace
leaned on by cypresses, but across his belly
a crack grinned hip to hip, and the right hand
lay palm-up in the dust. On the road back
I came on many such, but that was the first
of the cracked gods and the dusty altars.

I returned to the sea, and at the last mountain
I stood to remember, and the memory
could not live in the fact. I had grown old
in the wrong world. Penelope wove for nothing
her fabric and delay. I could not return.
I was woven to my dead men. In the dust
of the dead shore by the dead sea I lay down
and named their names who had matched lives with me,
and won. And they were all I loved.

Hawk-headed boys tilt for us in the sun.
A shoe of blood leaves footprints in wet sand,
printing a rose as fluent as the moon.
A green snout from the sea sniffs at the land.

A hand above the tarpits waves goodbye:
"Nice seeing you! I really hate to go!
If the hospitals are crowded, you and Vi
slip off and have the baby at the Zoo."

Surfs have been seen afire. At the last tide
Jones Beach blew higher than a Texas well.
The King of Rome woke and a certified
blank check from Heaven fluttered to his cell.

He spent it all and there was more on tap,
while the sad Khan to make his weight in jewels
ate lard and died, but, propped on his own lap,
sat up, even in death, to tip the scales.

Ten thousand teletypes stayed up all night
to track which way the wind was running out.
Dawn came up, breaking windows left and right.
"There's no such weather!" you said. Which I doubt.

Of Heroes Home from
Troy and More Coming

They were small ones, those camp-sung roar-boys
home god-sent from the cracked towns
and the runt-running ditches of the dead.
Brinebag pickled, deep-seized in their own noise
they were, but coasters at best, clowns
at worst, goat-scented in battle and bed.

Big words from the blood in the ram-banged
coast countries they knew; and an old
mad harpist sang what backyard forts
still ring to, though bloodless, in the spy-hanged
maples of summer play: an age told
in its own admiration, a sport of sorts.

Roped in scars, they homed and grew tall, retold,
as their own shadows shore-cast from prows.
Small they were, yes, a boy-race, but men, too,
the deaths they played with being god-grabbed old
as their blood's night-fit. It is death outgrows
these varsities, death alone they are seen through.

Take them for heroes, then, who drove
the straitway between bone grates
and what a man must be seen by.
They were noisy, yes, orators in love,
braggarts at war, poseurs at the seige gates,
cocksure of their kept goddess in the sky—

Yet to imagine such boys home, the race
polishes altars, crones call out together,
and grand-dads, leathered as Indians, nod
like wind-up toys on a back shelf of space.
Ah, how we wish to be beyond weather
and inconsolables, crazy for glory and God!

The Baboon and the State

A dog snout puzzles out the look of a man.
The wrong smell of a stranger tweaks the air.
"Fangs! Fangs! Why should we run? We are
Born of the chosen, first, and tallest tree!
Sons of the Sacred Banyan follow me!
Baboons are born to kill because they can."

Clemenceau said to the American
With the blue jaw and the fox-terrier hair,
"Above France, civilization." He made war
As if he strangled a mistress—tenderly,
But with a certain competence. A man
Must sacrifice for his own family.

Guido came trembling from the Vatican,
Roped up for God, God's moonspot in his hair.
"How shall I overthrow the Lateran?"
The Fat Pope said. "Speak up. God lives in me.
In His name teach me my cupidity."
And Guido spilled the malice in his ear.

Odysseus, that seven-minded man,
Piled up his kills to honor prophecy—
An indispensable, most Ithacan
Justification for a blood at war.
He spoke tongues and heard God-talk on the air,
But all his men were told was, "Follow me!"

Is man wrong for the State, or it for man?
High reasons and low causes make a war.

It is the Baboon kills, because he can
But Presidents hear voices from the air.
So packs and parishes cry equally:
"God's first and last Law sounded from a tree."

The voices come to rest where they began.
Clemenceau nods to the American.
Guido comes praying from the Vatican.
An indispensable most Ithacan
Baboon snout puzzles out the look of a man.
The killers kill. They kill because they can.

Captain Nicholas Strong

The moon with Venus in her sickle blade
made a masonic bangle in Orion,
then dimmed from gold to platinum in the haze,
not yet a dawn, that dusted up the sky
pale shade by shade, then dimmed again to pearl,
then sank into the ice-age before light,
shimmered from a blue depth, and, as a bird
skimmed on the surface, sank into the day.
Then the first fire ray shot above the earth.

All turned to day. Ambushed in history,
three guards on their last tower looked to the West
and saw it move, at first only a little.
A little was enough. The three descended,
opened the gate and waited, a white scarf
tied to a broomless broomstick. So it ended.
The trucks pulled in. A corporal took the guards
under his gun. The Captain called them up:
"Show us who's here." The three led through the yard;
but the thing had snapped already—like a dust
swirled forward by the wind, the corpses boiled
out of their graves and boxes, sullying
the light they moved in. With a shriek like joy,
but crazy, they blew past both armies, blind,
and crashed against a locked shed. As if noise
were force enough for all, the gray wall climbed,
the roof cracked, tilted, and the shed went over.
And there they clawed, each corpse mad with its find.
And when at last the Captain, forcing bone
apart from bone, got in to take a look,

he found it was flour-barrels, and the corpses
stood cramming flour into their mouths, both hands full,
and gagging as they swallowed, but still cramming,
choking and cramming, dying at last for food.

There was nothing else to do: he signaled back
for water, which was jostled to the ground,
and the dead men ate the paste out of their hands,
lay in it till they retched, and came unwound,
and let themselves be hauled away to life,
quivering and limp. And so within an hour
that, too, had ended, and some seemed to be
the parts of men again, if parts are men,
and if what men are parts of can be healed.
The Captain was no healer. He had wept
nothing in twenty years. He took two drinks
and shot the guards himself. And when the medics
arrived at last, he had no more to give,
and left the gates of Hell, sure he was right.
Still bleached with flour, pale as the day moon's finger,
he opened two more Hells before that night.

It takes no training to be dead. The Captain
was trapped in his own name—Nicholas Strong—
and made a muscle of it. Before he tracked
that shaved moon out, and, at the second dawn,
saw Venus drown alone, he had set free
six circles of the damned. What had he done
in all his life before that let him see
what he did now? He hated what he did—

their stink, their burls of bone, their slimey beards:
they clung to life so hard they dirtied it.
He would have shot them sooner than the guards
had he been God. The Captain had to kill:
only a violence could wash him. Sparks
shot from his hand, and part of every death
was that his face must never move.

                                   What part
of anything the Captain was in Hell
is all of us in time, I do not know.
In four moons more the Captain had undressed
from war forever. Home, and back again in
—of all things—Nick Strong's Haberdashery,
he dressed again, but never quite completely:
that day showed through no matter what he wore.
He knew it had meant something. Of his years
from dunes to bunkers, it was that first day
lurked in hat boxes and the racks of tweeds.
The Captain knew but never learned to say
he had been happiest when he stood most still,
letting one finger blast the world away,
carved like a rock and right, almost a will.
Grateful for what he killed, that being plain,
and loathing what he rescued, which, being sick,
troubled his health for mercies with no name.

The Gift

In 1945, when the keepers cried *kaput*,
Josef Stein, poet, came out of Dachau
like half a resurrection, his other
eighty pounds still in their invisible grave.

Slowly then the mouth opened and first
a broth, and then a medication, and then
a diet, and all in time and the knitting mercies,
the showing bones were buried back in flesh,

and the miracle was finished. Josef Stein,
man and poet, rose, walked, and could even
beget, and did, and died later of other causes
only partly traceable to his first death.

He noted—with some surprise at first—
that strangers could not tell he had died once.
He returned to his post in the library, drank his beer,
published three poems in a French magazine,

and was very kind to the son who at last was his.
In the spent of one night he wrote three propositions:
That Hell is the denial of the ordinary. That nothing lasts.
That clean white paper waiting under a pen

is the gift beyond history and hurt and heaven.

The Verbal Generation

As the hostess said,
it was really nothing,
and not even the flowers
bothered to nod
but posed,
cut and expensive,
between the martinis
and the elbows

after two hours of which
the author
and the painter
and the composer
and the poet
and the moderator

were taxied to the Hall
and went on stage
and talked
and answered questions
about being a generation.

Part III

CERTAINTIES

Homage to Lorca

Vivo estabas, Dios mio, dentro del ostensorio
punzando por tu Padre con agujas de lumbre.
Latiendo como el pobre corazón de la rana
que los médicos ponen en el frasco de vidrio.

García Lorca stood at the Spanish wall,
a world in his eyes. O frog's heart in the monstrance,
beating the specimen day of scientist Christ
as in a ray of light—the man is dead.

Fact, says the song of the dead man. Thus. So.
He is dead. I have no duty to say more.
The song does not transcend but signify
the fact of the man. The fact is he is dead

from the forced blood of his patience and impatience.
He is past the stab of light. He is sung to silence,
quick-limed to space, blown inward to a stone.
When the gunsights jumped, the mountains in his eyes

popped like balloons, the sky went out,
the wall could not hold him longer its own. What fell
with its terror steeled inside was Adam's all-
enduring son who in his body sang

man's mystery is to sweeten his own death.
Holding the world in his eyes, the son weeps true
from terror to himself. His love tells
the frog's heart beating yet in flasks of light,   69

fed by the saline wind, pumping from life
  the radiance of the animal in time
  touched by his torn and taken mercy.
  Give, says the song of the dead man. Touch. Feel.

(As in the Ghetto, when the Troopers called,
  the dead-already stripped and left their clothes
  to those who had not been called. A word was all:
  the fact of the name of the dead: the gift

of the rags of the dead to the shivering lives of men.)
  García Lorca stood in the Spanish fact
  stripped to his dark. O beating heart of the frog,
  the dead man's name is of the lighted blood.

A Thousandth Poem
for Dylan Thomas

Waking outside his Babylonian binge
   in the wet and cramp of morningstone, the sot
begins his daily death. A first stiff wince
   numbers his bones, each like a tooth of God.

Where did night end? Girlies in a red flame
   squeal through his broken memory like pigs:
Hell's barnyard burning or the zoo of days,
   stampeded shapes exploded from their skins.

He tastes again the ooze of a first sigh
   dead in his throat; his mouth, a rotten fig;
his sex, a broken glue-pot in the thighs;
   his breath, a shudder from below the will.

Sooner or later he must break an eye
   to look at what he sees of what he is.
An angel beating at the trap of time?
   A bird-heart pulsing in an idiot's fist?

Both. Either. Floated open from its muds,
   that moment in the clear, the sot's eye sees
as much as saints could bear of the fireblood
   God's heart pumps in its seizure of the skies.

Then how the man could sing his ghost to tears,
   there in God's eye and blood, for that lost place
where he was innocent, before his need
   changed to a thirst inside the worm of waste.   71

He pours his celebrations of regret,
    tormented joyous from the throat of mud,
hawk-hearted as Augustine in his sweat,
    dove-eyed as Francis' bridal with the wood.

It is the age of sots. Our holiness
    wakens outside the minareted fronts
of a jazzy, airless, and expensive hell.
    He sings our wish. He drinks his death for us

who have no throats to die of or to sing.
    He is Saint Binge at death in his own meat,
the blaze meant in the char we make of things,
    our addict, and our angel of defeat.

For Ezra Pound

not arrogant from habit
but furious from perception
Section: Rock Drill

Bagged for glory, then—a goat saint lolling
    satyr drunk and smiling loose-lipped
Heavens and Earths, the eyes rolling
    ecstasy and maunder, the beard flipped
to glory and the wattle visible under it. Die
    (giggle) dying (giggle) but not yet dead
(by a damn sight) not dead yet (sigh)
    but only cracked and queer with a head
full of the reasons for wine, that tomb-taste
    in the lees, a most like-life. And he fell
furious to perception. From the waist
    up, a Heaven. From the waist down, a Hell
too charred and sodden for riot, and so
    a kind of Heaven under, that Heaven above
being stormed and noisy as Hell. It is hard to know
    which dying takes a sot-saint's love.
To stink and look crazy and yet to groan
    from deep as the flesh is; that begins.
To burble bloody froths yet clown;
    that continues. To have two skins
on one back and be man and beast,
    that is nature in nature. To be is all.
To lie fervent as yeast
    at the root of bread and taste gall,
that is nature in an order not
    necessarily final but enduring. As catch can.   73

Saints are no bib-and-tucker. What
    do you think deaths are? The man
dies with his thoughts on, loused in his own
    stink, and bagged for Heaven burning.
O Reverend, of this hair and meat and bone
    render thy Christ his pomp and his returning.

Homage to Jacques Lipchitz

A child's face and man's it is,
staring through forests of statuary
with the look of the next thing in its eyes.

Fifty years of his own imagination
gather their shapes around him. The man enclosed
in what he has imagined encloses it.

Jacob Lipchitz, juif, fidèle à la foi
de ces ancêtres, a fait tout ça.
. . . Including a Virgin for Assy to hope

for what a man may say to the best in men.
Ten years in the making and still unfinished.
The bird hands still calling the dove down,

the man-mind still in love with one more
possibility beyond. It is no satyr
but a saint's intensity in joy walks there

calming that forest into imagination.
Do you need a way of saying "man"
there on 43rd St.? Twenty miles north

of business, in a stone garage by the Aqueduct
at Hastings-on-the-Hudson, he is saying it
shape by shape in that forest he makes and is—

the child's face and the man's that will do
for every creed to turn to for answers
should the God in all their books one day ask,

"What have I done that tells and justifies?"

Some Figures for Who Must Speak

i

Forget understanding. There will be none.
A condition natural as weather is between us.
Our lives are in separate airs. Our memories
are seas and mountains: sometimes and for a while
in sight of one another, but across an element.

You mountain Congregationalists—will you believe
however faithfully at every risk
I dredge it from myself, the existence of squid?
I carry an oar on my shoulder, and who
in all these uplands knows it moves a world?

You sea-going mackerel snatchers by the sputtery pumps—
would you answer, though I break my back for it,
to September hay sweated from ledges
in the sight of four weathers at once
there in the sluices and bowls below my footing?

Whatever is, is the natural day of who goes there.

ii

It takes a habit of living. Poetry
is the family talk of the generations:
you have to have lived in the house of that name.

When an outsider happens in, it stops or changes.
The young, being someways truest, prattle
to confuse him. The old may try, for politeness,

to say a little something. But whatever
was going on there round the table,
or by the fire, or squealing through the hall,

dressing, undressing, and piggy-back to bed—
whatever was going on before the stranger
came popping smalltalk from somewherever else—

the faces sit re-arranged and the fun is over.

iii

Is it possible to say it without memories?
As if in answer to a questionnaire? squared
like columns in a statistician's eye?

It is a plain thing. Plain enough for saying.
A white elk, for that matter, once you come on it,
is as visible as a jackass: there it is.

The trick is to happen next to it and
to be ready for what happens. I've known men
to see that elk and think it was a ground fog.

It is a plain thing, then, but one must have eyes.
I can see it as it is: I cannot name it
by any names you know. "Poetry," I say,

and you think of Longfellow, and I
of the race in its going: the family at its days:

the young at the edge of the thicket where the elk sleeps.

I mean the thing behind the name of the thing.

iv

Perhaps it could start with an exchange of pictures:
you may think of me as a knob-kneed wheezy paunch
too old to hunt, but left on guard at the cavemouth.

(There is more to it than that, but that will do.
I sit here watching the cubs spill in the sun,
and think: "Tonight I shall try again to carve an Elk head."

It is something to think about, a way
of leaving that much of myself to the cave forever—
if I can truly remember the lines of that head.)

You are also a man of intentions. I see you
(you must not let the change of time and scene
confuse you: this is all times and all scenes:

I speak for the family in all its ages)
—I see you also as the keeper of a propriety,
both in your nakedness, and naked but wearing a collar.

You are something and believe something (that
is not necessarily the same thing). And you distrust me
with your certainties. I waste the family's time.

It was so I met you once in Florida
in the image of a Baptist graduate student
who told me that the Absolute in Aesthetics

was the same as the Absolute in everything else.
When I asked what that might be, he tossed his mane,
and pointing his finger and his whole arm, said:

"The Triune God!"—Now suppose you're as saved as he is
(as all of you are somewhere inside yourselves)
how shall I not be read in your own image?

And how shall I carve that Elk's head
which is the Elk's head truly remembered? the presence
of life in the thicket named for my hunting tribe?

the picture of themselves my people are?

V

It can also be half-seen half-truly.
I could show you what an elk is.
Even what a white elk is. But can I
show you, or you see, the elk in his stance?
musky and rank in the great steam of his presence?

It is in the elk and equally in the life
of the elk people that the seeing happens.
After the first son who was killed in the hunt
was buried with the elk's horns on his cairn,
we tore the flesh of the beast hot from the fire.

vi

It can also be half-said half-truly.
But remember of what is half-said
that it must be twice heard: once
in the words of the saying, and again
in the burial and the feast between two bloods.

I am, for plainness, a tribesman speaking
to other councils. "See what a land of plenty
we war in," I say. "Let us possess our difference
and hunt our need in peace, to die as that first son
at whose grave we wintered; not in these games of stones."

And there you sit in your feathers and Absolutes,
pointing your finger and arm. Do I see three heads
thrown back? Well then, the pow-wow is ended.
Your people are not mine. And yet, whoever
wins this war must hunt that Elk or starve.

A Praise of Good Poets
in a Bad Age

To the memory of
Wallace Stevens

Any man—God, if he had the money—
could rip the sagebrush back for terraced gardens
and tilt a pearlstone Hollywood between
the swimming pools and the Pacific.

Lord, what we know of doing badly!
the nerve's reach for order gone huge,
eye-catching, and moneyed. How shall I say this right
who say "Lord" and mean something else?—

Something not Heaven nor Hell, but something.
The tongue is wrong in the mouth to say it, the words
soggy from the prayers of lace-curtain angels.
We lack a vocabulary for admiration.

And still a man could take a train to magnificence:
to Rutherford for Williams, to Hartford for Stevens,
to Cambridge for Frost—and not have it, and yet
have touched the most of it in one day's going.

How much higher in its own mind could the age stand
than these three have stood for it?
Now Stevens is dead from meaning-as-it-is,
and that day's ride to the age's best

longer by an absence as it goes shortened
by stone imagined forests of stopped birds

81

and voices windborne from a midnight river,
an oarlock's birdcall from the gist of time.

Imagine any man at that train's windows,
watching the world from this death and these lives,
hearing the carried voice of their alert—
what shall defend Newark from his arrival?

Harlem from his revulsion? South Station from his defeat?
Once in Connecticut from such a window
I saw three egrets statued by marsh-reaches
as if posed for the eyes of Egyptian lovers.

What a suave possibility they made of the sky!
But before the next-to-prayer in my heart could open
we broke the soot of Somewhere-on-the-Line
and my eye crashed like a flung egg on its walls.

Is it a symptom only or a source,
that permission of ugliness in American houses?
Arson could be a creed, and a vote for Nero
a vote for a compassionate corruption.

Call the dead poet from his imaginings:
"*Soit!*" he chimes back from that pixie passion
that made his belltowers tinkle as they bonged.
"*Waa-waallee-waa!*" the whistle learns to say.

Nonsense. But nearer than the age to being.
It is no chin-thrust figure angel-high

the ardent man lifts from his ordering:
leave those grim doughboys to the yokel squares.

By bong and tinkle he dwarfed back the fronts
of the age's skew and sooty imagination.
Now he is dead: one gone of the three truest,
and poverty, drowned in money, cannot care.

Soit! To be a poet in an age of prose
is to hear more than the age is ready for.
Caroo, Caballero! the States lack word of cockles.
A bronze pear hanging is not news enough

now Congress has the language by the throat.
Let it strut for nothing. "Fat! Fat! Fat! Fat!"
When the age has found a memory near enough
his news from bronze, most houses will come down.

To W. T. Scott

with thanks for a poem

I like that poem, Win. There's a green world in it.
Not just green acreage—any nature boy
can rhyme on that a dozen lines a minute:
put in a bluebird if you're out for joy,
put in a hayloft if you're out for plot,
put in a dead tree if you're out for thought.

I mean what's green in being what a man
touches to leave. Say, Mark Twain at the end;
the green of his last thought. Suppose it ran
to Huck or Jim drifting around a bend;
then stopped there with a sigh or with a smile,
or even wondering had it been worthwhile,

but still a life to think about that stood
green to itself. As God might lose a world
yet think back and be sad that it was good.
All green dies. But the sere manfingers curled
to their last pulse, touch in a memory.
Touch, and I think are justified. For me

that green is first. The green thought more than green
of Walden is Thoreau. The man unspared.
As queer as he was green. An in-between:
half-Cod, half-Buddha. But a system bared
to its own pulse. He had a mind with wings.
But best of all he had an eye for things.

God, how he could see green! He must have died
with time ablaze around him like spring fern
caught in a single ray of sun inside
a glacier-rumpled Stonehenge, while a churn
of swallows buttered him his last of light.
—All nothing till he held it in his sight.

That green. Say, Whitman like a stricken bear
thinking: "What is a sea?" Say, Henry James
thinking: "What country is it over there?"
on a long foggy walk beside the Thames.
Say, Melville thinking: "What have I left done
that will stay green to time for anyone?"

And *all* done. What a sea or country is.
What world can grow to, shaped round from the mind.
Such forests deeper than Yosemites
a man walks thinking in and leaves behind.
That last green, Win, after the first unrolled.
The eighth day of the world, by a man told.

An Inscription for
Richard Eberhart

I do not intend the people I know to believe me
outside themselves: belief is inside the self.
"It is the not-me in my friend delights me,"
Emerson wrote. It is my friend in me
that lets me see my friend.—These are convictions
one sleep this side of poetry. But in time,
with sleep dissolving from me like a mist,
I find the shape of a scimitar still in my hand
and know what holy wars I should have gone to
in the right season. When I say to my friends:
"We are that invisible war," they smile
with a smile I know from myself. It is so we learn,
one from another, our difference is no war
but the delicate jointure of the parts of a skull.

But is the articulation of bones a meeting?
I have slept on ruined Rome and wakened green
with the squeal of birds and the power-hum of the bees
sealed in the air like amber. In the atrium,
a laborer was eating bread and cheese
in the noonday of his wine. I watched his ease.
It was longer than the ruin. "*Buon appetito!*"
I cried like God in the Sunday of my pleasure.
He raised his wine flask and called back "*Salute!*"
Then did he turn to stone? Or the stones to him?
Something stayed fixed in time out of that meeting:
a signal from my friend in me, a placement
of holy banquets in their atrium,
a vision of the bones that speak themselves.

DATE DUE